D0384552

MONUMENTAL MILESTONES
GREAT EVENTS OF MODERN TIMES

Blitzkrieg!
Hitler's
Lightning War

German dictator Adolf Hitler ignited a
lightning war in 1939 and conquered most of
Western Europe.

Mitchell Lane
PUBLISHERS

Hockessin, Delaware 19707

Titles in the Series

Blitzkrieg!
Hitler's
Lightning War

The pain of war: A Sudeten woman reluctantly hails German occupiers with the Nazi salute in 1938.

Earle Rice Jr.

Printing   1   2   3   4   5   6   7   8   9

Library of Congress Cataloging-in-Publication Data
Rice, Earle.
   Blitzkrieg! Hitler's lightning war / by Earle Rice Jr.
       p. cm. — (Monumental milestones)
   Includes bibliographical references and index.
   ISBN 978-1-58415-542-3 (library bound : alk. paper)
   1. World War, 1939–1945—Germany. 2. World War, 1939–1945—Campaigns—Europe. 3. World War, 1939–1945—Campaigns—Africa, North. 4. Hitler, Adolf, 1889–1945. 5. Germany—History—1933–1945. I. Title.
D757.R48 2007
940.54'0943—dc22

                                                 2007023408

ABOUT THE AUTHOR: Earle Rice Jr. is a former senior design engineer and technical writer in the aerospace, electronic-defense, and nuclear industries. He has devoted full time to his writing since 1993 and is the author of more than fifty published books. Earle is listed in *Who's Who in America* and is a member of the Society of Children's Book Writers and Illustrators; the League of World War I Aviation Historians and its UK-based sister organization, Cross & Cockade International; the United States Naval Institute; the Air Force Association; and the Disabled American Veterans.

PHOTO CREDITS: Cover, p. 16—Hulton Archive/Getty Images; pp. 1, 6, 25—Library of Congress; pp. 3, 12, 20, 24, 36, 38—National Archives; p. 14—Neils Bosboom; p. 18—Gregory J. W. Urwin Collection; p. 26 map—Sharon Beck; pp. 27, 39—Army Military.

Contents

Blitzkrieg! Hitler's Lightning War

Earle Rice Jr.

*For Your Information

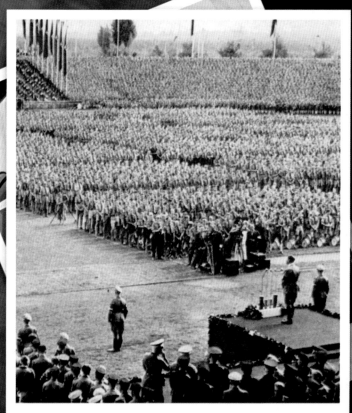

Nazi Party rally in Nuremberg, 1938. Nazi Party rallies began in 1923.

Hitler staged these martial spectacles to arouse the emotions of the German people and gain support for himself and Nazism. They grew into annual events, with each new rally becoming grander than the previous one. The Nazis held their last rally in 1938.

Resurrection

"Today Germany is ours, and tomorrow the whole world,"[1] declared Adolf Hitler to the German people. As the leader of the National Socialist Party—the Nazis—he rose to power in the 1930s. He promised to make Germany a powerful force in the world. At the same time, the German dictator assured the rest of the world of his desire for peace.

In September 1938, he spoke to a gathering of Hitler Youth at the Nazi Party rally in Nuremberg. "You, my youth," Hitler said, "are our nation's most precious guarantee for a great future and you are destined to be the leaders of a glorious new order under the supremacy of National Socialism. Never forget that one day you will rule the world."[2]

While the world slept, German factories built tanks, guns, and warplanes—and the German army grew larger and stronger. Hitler talked of peace, but he prepared for war. By 1939, all he needed was an excuse to start one. In August of that year, he told his generals, "I shall give a propagandist reason for starting the war, whether it is plausible or not. . . . In starting and waging a war it is not Right that matters, but Victory."[3]

On the last night of August 1939, a small band of soldiers stormed the German radio station at Gleiwitz (now Gliwice, Poland), about a mile from the Polish border. The soldiers wore Polish uniforms and sported Polish-style mustaches and sideburns. They were led by Major Alfred Naujocks of the *Sicherheitsdienst*, or SD—the German security service.

The raiders shot up the station and broadcast an appeal to the Polish people: "The time has come for war between Poland and Germany! Unite and smash down any German, all Germans, who oppose your war. . . . The time has come!"[4] The "Polish" raiders quickly fled. They left behind the dead body of a

condemned prisoner from a German concentration camp. The prisoner had been killed earlier and dressed in a Polish uniform to make it appear that the attackers were Polish.

While the Germans were faking their attack at Gleiwitz, other SD soldiers were staging similar assaults on a forestry station and a customs building on the German side of the border. They left behind several more dead bodies in Polish uniforms, code-named "canned goods." Hitler had his excuse to start a war.

At four-thirty on the morning of September 1, 1939, German shots rang out and German bombs began to drop along the frontier in Poland. Fifteen minutes later, the aging German battleship *Schleswig-Holstein* opened fire on a Polish munitions depot in Danzig (now Gdańsk, Poland) harbor. Later that morning, Hitler addressed the nation from the Reichstag (German parliament) in Berlin. "This night for the first time Polish regular soldiers fired on our own territory," he said. "Since 5:45 A.M. [actually 4:45 A.M.] we have been returning the fire, and from now on bombs will be met with bombs."[5] World War II had begun.

While Hitler was speaking, 1.5 million troops in five armies of the German Wehrmacht (armed forces) were surging across the Polish frontier. They thrust hard, fast, and deep into the Polish heartland on an eastward dash toward the Polish capital of Warsaw. The Poles could muster fewer than a million men to check the swarm of Hitler's onrushing attackers.

On September 3, Great Britain and France—who had both signed a treaty to aid Poland in the event of such an attack—declared war on Germany. Unfortunately for Poland, they stood by impotently and watched the ensuing rout unfold.

In the early phase of the German offensive, some 1,500 dive-bombers and fighter planes of the Luftwaffe (German air force) blackened the skies over Poland. They bombed Polish air bases and shot Polish planes out of the air in droves. In only a few days, the Polish air force ceased to exist as an effective fighting force. With control of the air, Luftwaffe aircraft flew in support of ground operations. In many instances, shrieking gull-winged Stuka dive-bombers acted as long-range artillery, bombing Polish towns and cities at will.

German tanks—mostly Panzer IIIs—whined and streaked across Poland at dazzling speeds. (*Panzer* is the German word for "armor" and is usually taken to mean "tank.") By September 7, the highly mechanized German lead forces had reached a point within twenty-five miles of the Polish capital.

Ten days later, on September 17, most of the Polish Army found itself encircled. As the Poles tried to break out on the River Bzura, the Germans contained them and crushed them. That same day, Soviet forces (who were briefly allied with the Germans) invaded Poland from the east. Poland's fate was sealed. Warsaw fell to the Germans on September 27. In less than a month, the Polish campaign was effectively over.

A correspondent for *Time* magazine gave a name to the opening phase of World War II. He aptly described the hostilities in Poland as "no war of occupation, but a war of quick penetration and obliteration—*Blitzkrieg*—lightning war."[6] The name stuck.

~

The world looked on in amazement as Hitler's war machine toppled Poland. Observers spoke in awe of a new kind of warfare—mechanized, lightning fast, and devastating. But the concept of blitzkrieg was not new. Although the term comes from two German words—*Blitz* (lightning) and *Krieg* (war)—the origins of this type of fighting are not German.

"In the broadest sense, this was warfare as it had been waged by Alexander the Great, Genghis Khan, and Napoleon," wrote Trevor N. Dupuy, a noted military analyst and career officer in the U.S. Army, "modified only to make use of the latest products of science and technology."[7] In terms of modern warfare, many historians credit the writings of British military theorists J.F.C. Fuller and B. H. Liddell Hart for first putting forth the precepts of lightning war.

As a high-level tank officer in World War I, then-Colonel J.F.C. Fuller was putting together a plan for the first true tank offensive in 1918. It was called Plan 1919. It called for the use of tanks en masse as a strike force rather than widely separated as infantry-support weapons. Before the British Tank Corps could carry out his plan, the war ended. British Army leaders shelved Fuller's revolutionary concept, and Plan 1919 went nowhere.

Liddell Hart was a military journalist and retired army captain. In the 1920s, he argued that the development of the tank and the airplane enabled rapid movement. Mobility, in turn, might alter the World War I concept of fixed front lines. "In most campaigns," he wrote, "dislocation of the enemy's psychological and physical balance has been the vital prelude to a successful attempt at his overthrow."[8]

In 1927, the British War Office authorized an Experimental Mechanized Force. Its weapons budget was small, however, and the cost of building tanks was high. The British Army moved painfully slowly toward acting on the tank theories of Fuller and Liddell Hart. In France, Colonel (later General) Charles de Gaulle championed the concentrated use of armor and aircraft as offensive weapons. His urgings fell on the deaf ears of French defense-minded war planners.

German military thinkers, on the other hand, paid close attention to the armored warfare writings of the British and the French. They built on them with lessons learned from their own experiences in World War I. They soon moved past their old enemies in the development of principles for coordinated infantry-armor and air-armor operations. When set in motion, these principles took on the modern name of *blitzkrieg*. In simple terms, blitzkrieg is the military tactic of combining swiftly moving ground forces with devastating air attacks to defeat an enemy. It uses the elements of surprise, lightning-fast speed, deep penetration, and encirclement to cut off and destroy or force the surrender of enemy forces.

In the two decades following its humiliating defeat in World War I, Germany gradually rebuilt an army second to none in the world. It did so under the leadership and guidance of such noteworthy generals as Hans von Seeckt, Heinz Guderian, and Erwin Rommel. Under the supreme command of Adolf Hitler, the German army overwhelmed Poland in a month. Hitler took full credit for the victory and turned his eyes toward Western Europe. The resurrected German army would take him there.

"Hans von Seeckt was the core of the effort to rebuild and reform the German army, and a major share of the result should be credited to him."[9] So writes military historian James S. Corum in *The Roots of Blitzkrieg*.

Born into a noble Prussian military family in Schleswig, Germany, on April 22, 1866, von Seeckt rose rapidly in the German army. He served in top-level staff positions in World War I. After the war, Lieutenant General von Seeckt was named senior military adviser to the German delegation at Versailles (vurr-SIGH), France. He became a leading authority on the requirements of the Treaty of Versailles, the agreement that ended World War I. The treaty abolished Germany's air force and imposed strict limits on the size, makeup, and arms of its army and navy.

Hans von Seeckt

In July 1919, von Seeckt was appointed chief of the troop office of the Army Command. He became responsible for planning a 100,000-man army and supervising its training. Despite the limitations of the Versailles Treaty, von Seeckt rebuilt the small postwar German army into a nucleus for later expansion in the Hitler era. He set high standards for personnel, training, and maneuvers. By working secretly within the Soviet Union to train German tank and aircraft crews, he successfully skirted the restrictions of Versailles.

In 1921, von Seeckt documented his military theories in *Command of Combined Arms Combat*. This collection of his field service regulations became a classic work of military doctrine. It provided a blueprint for blitzkrieg and the operational and tactical success of the Wehrmacht during the early phases of World War II.

Von Seeckt retired in 1926 but returned to active military life in 1934. He journeyed to China to assist in the training of the Chinese Army of Chiang Kai-shek's Nationalist government. Von Seeckt did much to modernize the Chinese Army. The Chinese troops he helped to train put up a solid resistance against the Japanese invaders in the late 1930s. Von Seeckt, whom many think of as the "architect" of the German army, died in Berlin in 1936.

British and French soldiers were taken prisoner in France in 1940.

Hitler's armies swept through the Low Countries and France in the spring of 1940. In defeat, French losses alone totaled an estimated 90,000 dead, 200,000 wounded, and 1.9 million taken prisoner. Some 338,000 British, French, and Belgian troops escaped death or capture in the remarkable evacuation of Dunkirk, France.

Operation Yellow and the Fall of France

After Germany's whirlwind defeat of Poland in September 1939, World War II settled into an odd lull until the following spring. In German terms, *Blitzkrieg* (lightning war) gave way to *Sitzkrieg* (sitting war). The French called the six-month period of calm *la drôle de guerre* (the Phony War). Britain and France were in no hurry to rush into war. Moreover, many German generals felt that their armies were not yet prepared for a major action. Mostly, however, the long lull was because of poor weather conditions. Tanks and aircraft cannot operate efficiently, if at all, in bad weather.

But a war without conflict could not last for long. Neither could Hitler long refrain from exhibiting his newly vetted war machine to Western Europe.

On April 9, 1940, Hitler's armies again shattered Europe's calm with the invasion of Denmark and Norway. Denmark fell to the Wehrmacht's lightning-like assault in only twenty-four hours; Norway, in twenty-three days. Despite these successes, Denmark and Norway were only stops along the way in Hitler's plan called *Fall Gelb* (Case Yellow). As far back as October 1939, Hitler had issued a war directive authorizing attacks on the Low Countries and France:

> I have decided, without further loss of time, to go over to the offensive. Any further delay will not only entail the end of Belgian and perhaps of Dutch neutrality, to the advantage of the Allies [chiefly Britain and France, and later the Soviet Union and the United States], but it will also increasingly strengthen the military power of the enemy, reduce the confidence of the

neutral nations in Germany's final victory, and make it more difficult to bring Italy as a full ally into the war.[1]

Case (or Operation) Yellow called for a resumption of Hitler's blitz-krieg tactics in the Low Countries—Belgium, Holland, and Luxembourg—and in France. German Army Group B under General Fedor von Bock was to launch a powerful but limited assault on the Low Countries. At the same time, Army Group A led by General Gerd von Rundstedt would launch the main German thrust through the hilly Ardennes region of Belgium, Luxembourg, and northeastern France. Meanwhile, General Wilhelm von Leeb's Army Group C would hold the front line along the Rhine River opposite France's Maginot (MAH-zhee-noh) Line. (The Maginot Line was a complex system of fortifications that ran along France's eastern frontier from Montmédy to Switzerland.) Operation Yellow commenced on May 10, 1940.

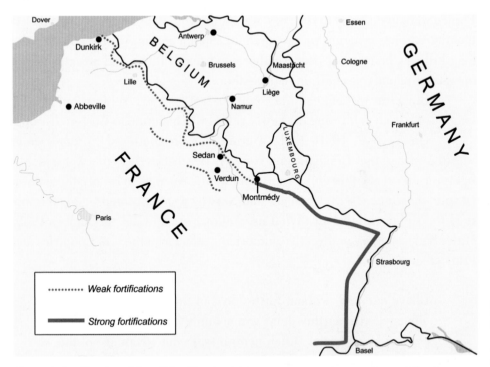

Map of the Maginot Line. The Maginot Line was a complex system of fortresses that were linked by pill boxes, minefields, zigzagging barbed wire, and tank traps. The line stretched from Montmédy, France, to the Swiss border.

On that same day, Winston Churchill replaced Neville Chamberlain as Britain's prime minister. Three days later, he told the House of Commons, "I have nothing to offer but blood, toil, tears, and sweat."[2] Churchill and the British people would need plenty of each in the troubled days ahead. Hitler's panzer divisions, led by Generals Erwin Rommel and Heinz Guderian, had already crossed the Meuse River at Dinant, Belgium, and Sedan, France.

Luxembourg had no defense forces and offered no resistance. The Dutch blew up bridges across key rivers and mined canals in eastern Holland to slow the German advance. They opened water gates in a network of dikes to flood vast areas to little avail. German paratroopers struck deep into Holland. Luftwaffe aircraft heavily bombed Rotterdam. Dutch resistance collapsed before help from the British and French could arrive. To spare the Hague and other cities from bombings, Holland surrendered after five days.

Belgian forces put up a stiffer defense. They took up positions behind the Albert Canal. Fort Eben Emael guarded the junction of the canal and the Meuse River and anchored their defense line. German airborne troops reached the canal's bridges before the Belgians could destroy them. Glider-borne troops landed on the roof of the seemingly impregnable fortress. Explosive charges dropped through observation slits silenced the guns of Eben Emael. Mechanized German forces of Army Group B swept across Belgium under cover of supporting Messerschmitt Me (Bf) 109 fighters, Junkers Ju-87 Stuka dive-bombers, and Junkers Ju-88 medium bombers. Belgian forces fought hard but could not match the force of German arms. Belgium surrendered on May 28.

Meanwhile, to the south, German panzer units of Army Group A skirted the Maginot Line and roared through the Ardennes. The French thought the hills and gullies of the densely wooded region would make the Ardennes impassable to tanks. They were wrong. German infantry poured through the "Panzer Corridor" and held it while German tanks crossed the Meuse at Sedan and elsewhere.

To help stem the flow of tanks into France, 170 French and British bombers—100 of them Bristol Blenheims—tried to knock out the Gaulier Bridge at Sedan. Major Johann Kielmansegg, of Heinz Guderian's XIX Panzer Corps, described the Allied air attack:

Junkers JU-87 dive-bombers were more popularly known as Stukas.

Stuka *is an abbreviation for* Sturzkampfflug- zeug, *the German word for "dive- bomber." Famous for its gull-wings and shrieking engine, the Stuka was highly effective in actions against ground troops and tanks in Europe and North Africa.*

The summer landscape with the quietly flowing river, the light green of the meadows bordered by the darker summits of the more distant heights, spanned by a brilliantly blue sky, is filled with the racket of war. For hours at a time, the dull explosions of bombs, the quick tack-tack of the machine guns . . . mingles with the droning of the aircraft motors and the roar of the division passing over the bridge unimpeded. . . . Again and again, an enemy aircraft crashes out of the sky, dragging a long black plume of smoke behind it.[3]

Major Kielmansegg watched from the bridge as eleven enemy planes crashed in barely an hour. The British lost forty-five of their bombers; the French lost five. Guderian's panzers rumbled on across northwestern France,

depending on speed to protect their flanks. They reached the English Channel at Abbeville on May 21. Their drive extended the Panzer Corridor to the Channel, cutting the Allied armies in two and isolating a large pocket of British and French troops near the French port of Dunkirk.

Heinz Guderian was one of the first Germans to recognize the potential of armor (chiefly tanks) in modern warfare. Many historians call him the "father of Blitzkrieg." In the 1920s, he studied the works of British and French armor theorists and built on them. By 1928, he had developed his own theories for employing tanks en masse in combined-arms attacks. He rehearsed his theories in peacetime maneuvers and wrote about them in his book *Achtung! Panzer* (*Attention! Armor*) in 1937. In the campaigns for Poland and France, Guderian led his armor into action and proved the deadly efficiency of his ideas.

North of Sedan, France, another panzer leader was trying out his skills for the first time. As commander of the 7th Panzer Division since February 1940, Major General Erwin Rommel was new to armored command. But the decorated infantry officer of World War I was a quick learner. After crossing the Meuse at Dinant, Rommel led his panzers across Flanders in a blazing assault. Moving faster and farther than any other division in military history, Rommel's panzers became known as the "Ghost" or "Phantom" division. They seemed to appear out of nowhere, spreading confusion and terror everywhere. On May 20, Rommel reached Arras and turned northeast toward Lille, southeast of Dunkirk, arriving there on May 26.

That night, Rommel wrote in his diary: "The worst is well over. There's little likelihood of any more hard fighting, for we've given the enemy a proper towsing [rumpling]."[4] Hitler awarded Rommel the Knight's Cross—the highest degree of the Iron Cross—for his valor during the armored drive across Belgium and France.

Two days earlier, with most of the German armor massed for attack against the southern perimeter of the Dunkirk pocket, Hitler ordered the panzers to halt. He wanted to allow time for the infantry and other slower units to catch up with the fast-moving tankers. His decision turned out to be one of many errors of judgment he would commit over the course of World War II. During the forty-eight-hour lull provided by Hitler's much-criticized "Halt Order,"

Erwin Rommel (left) with captured British officers in Cherbourg, France, June 1940.

The former infantry officer earned a medal and a promotion as a new tank commander during the fighting against France. Rommel later became famous as the "Desert Fox" in North Africa.

the Allies threw up defenses around Dunkirk and prepared plans for an evacuation that was to follow from May 26 to June 3 (see FYI: Dunkirk).

After the historic evacuation at Dunkirk, the Germans turned south to deal with the remnants of the French Army. In June, dispirited French divisions fell back mile after mile before the German onslaught. The French tried to set up a defense line to protect Paris and the interior, but the Germans sliced through their lines and forced the surrender of some 400,000 French troops. Italian dictator Benito Mussolini, convinced of a German victory, launched an invasion on southern France on June 10. Paris fell on June 14.

The Germans pressed on and captured Lyon on June 20. Marshal Philippe Pétain, France's newly installed prime minister, called for the guns to fall silent. Pétain, a hero of World War I, signed a humiliating armistice with the Germans at Compiègne (kohmp-YEN) on June 22. France had fallen to Hitler's brand of lightning warfare in just over five weeks. Operation Yellow ended in a shocking German victory.

FYInfo

FOR YOUR INFORMATION

After reaching Abbeville near the English Channel, General Heinz Guderian's XIX Panzer Corps turned north and swept up the French coastline. His panzers isolated the French port of Boulogne (boo-LOHN) on May 21, 1940, and the port of Calais (kaa-LAY) the next day. Dunkirk became the only port left open to the Allies. On May 24, Guderian stood poised to attack Dunkirk. Some of his panzers had already crossed the Allied canal defense line about ten miles from Dunkirk. Suddenly—and unexpectedly—the German High Command ordered its armored forces to halt. Hitler himself confirmed the order.

Scholars cite several possible reasons for the controversial order. Army Group A commander Gerd von Rundstedt wanted to rest and reassemble his armies before pressing the attack, and some advisers had warned Hitler against the use of tanks in the often muddy areas of Flanders. Moreover, Luftwaffe

General Heinz Guderian

chief Hermann Göring had assured him that the German air force could easily finish off any isolated British and Belgian forces. Others suggest that Hitler had held back in hopes of negotiating favorable peace terms with Britain later. Whatever Hitler's reasons were, his decision may have cost him any chance of winning the war.

The German advance stopped for two—almost three—days. During the lull in the fighting, Lord John Gort, commander of the British Expeditionary Force (BEF), used the time to erect an effective defense ring at Dunkirk. At the same time, Admiral Sir Bertram Ramsay gathered every available seacraft to rescue Allied troops stranded along a ten-mile stretch of beach at Dunkirk. The makeshift fleet consisted of destroyers, fishing boats, ferries, yachts, motorboats, and more.

Evacuations began on May 28 and continued into June 4. Under an umbrella of Royal Air Force (RAF) Spitfires and Hurricanes, the odd mix of Allied vessels rescued some 338,000 British, French, and Belgian troops who lived to fight another day. Göring's vaunted Luftwaffe met their match in the RAF, losing 240 aircraft in nine days. The heavily outnumbered RAF lost 177.

In 1939, dictators Adolf Hitler (rig
Mussolini formed an alliance between t
nations of Germany and Italy.

Their alliance was known as the Pact of Steel. A year later, Germany, Italy, and Japan signed the Tripartite Pact, calling for the three nations to provide mutual military assistance. The trio became known as the Axis nations, a term describing the enemies of the Allies.

The Desert Fox in North Africa

After France fell in June 1940, Hitler's offensive in Western Europe stopped at land's end. The Wehrmacht paused to prepare for Hitler's next move—the invasion of England. Hitler called his invasion plan Operation Sea Lion. He advised his Italian ally Benito Mussolini of his plan. Mussolini felt that the time was right to expand his Libyan colony in North Africa. On August 19, he sent a message to Marshal Rodolfo Graziani, commander in chief of Italian forces in North Africa: "Now, on the day on which the first platoon of German soldiers lands on British soil, you too will attack."[1]

In the summer and fall of 1940, the Royal Air Force turned back the Luftwaffe in the Battle of Britain. The RAF victory forced Hitler to scrap Operation Sea Lion. Despite the German setback, Mussolini sent five divisions about sixty-five miles into British-held Egypt and captured the coastal village of Sidi Barrani. Although Italian forces in North Africa outnumbered British troops by 200,000 to 40,000, British raiders of General Archibald Wavell's Western Desert Force retook Sidi Barrani on December 9. The British also seized 38,800 Italian prisoners, including four generals. "Something is wrong with our Army," Italian minister of foreign affairs Count Galeazzo Ciano noted in his diary, "if five divisions allow themselves to be pulverized in two days."[2] And the worst was yet to come.

The British turned the Sidi Barrani raid into a full-scale offensive. Continuing westward, they captured the entire Libyan province of Cyrenaica (sihr-uh-NAY-uh-kuh) and captured another 130,000 Italian prisoners. Mussolini appealed to his friend Hitler for help. Hitler called on newly promoted Lieutenant General Erwin Rommel to right the wrong alluded to by Count Ciano. "In view of the highly critical situation with our Italian allies, two German divisions—one light and one panzer—were to be sent to Libya to

their help," Rommel wrote later. "I was to take command of this German Afrika Korps and was to move off as soon as possible to Libya."[3]

Rommel flew into Tripoli, the capital of Libya, on February 14, 1941. His orders called for him to remain on the defensive. On paper, Rommel reported to an Italian general; in practice, he operated pretty much on his own. In March, contrary to his orders, he led the fast-moving Afrika Korps and several added Italian divisions in a blistering blitzkrieg campaign against British forces. He wasted little time in recovering Mussolini's losses. By mid-April, his forces had taken back all of the lost land except for Tobruk.

The British had not expected a German counterattack until June, but Rommel had "outfoxed" them. His brash action and cunning earned him the nickname of "Desert Fox."

Tobruk, Libya, was a tiny coastal town of 4,000 people, but it was the only decent port between Tripoli and Alexandria, Egypt. Both sides wanted it as a source for supplies. In a clear message to General Wavell, Winston Churchill wrote, "Tobruk, therefore, seems to be a place to be held to the death, without thought of retirement."[4] Some 30,000 British and Australian defenders resisted Rommel's repeated attacks. Tobruk held. Rommel bypassed it and advanced to Halfaya Pass in Egypt.

In May and June 1941, he beat back two British counterattacks, but short supplies were becoming a problem. On June 22, 1941, Hitler launched Operation Barbarossa, the invasion of the Soviet Union. Hitler's new offensive drew off arms and supplies that otherwise might have gone to Rommel. In November, a third British offensive forced him back into Libya, but not for long. His Afrika Korps was strengthened by reinforcements and fresh supplies and was upgraded as the German-Italian Panzer Army, or *Panzerarmee*. He resumed the seesaw desert war in January 1942.

Rommel drove eastward in another desert-style blitzkrieg to the Gazala Line. The line was a zone of fortified "boxes" linked by minefields. It extended from the Mediterranean port of Gazala to a southern strongpoint at Bir Hacheim (bihr-hah-KAYM).

With his latest offensive, Rommel's reputation as the Desert Fox continued to grow. Hitler promoted Rommel to the rank of colonel (full) general.

He also awarded him the Swords to the Oak Leaves of the Knight's Cross. (Swords and Oak Leaves denote higher orders of the original medal.)

On May 26 at 10:30 P.M., Rommel sent a small force to feint an attack on the center of the British Eighth Army's Gazala Line. (The Eighth Army was an outgrowth of the Western Desert Force.). At the same time, he circled around the southern end of the line with his main force of some 10,000 vehicles. He planned to seize Bir Hacheim, knock off the string of strong boxes one by one, and mount an assault on Tobruk in a northward sweep. After three weeks of intense desert fighting, he did just that. On June 17, Rommel captured a huge British supply dump east of Tobruk. Four days later, Tobruk and its 30,000 defenders finally fell to elements of Rommel's Panzer Army.

"The booty was gigantic," Rommel's chief of staff declared later. "It consisted of supplies for 30,000 men for three months."[5] Hitler promoted Rommel to field marshal for his remarkable achievement. At age forty-nine, Rommel had become the youngest—and the most famous—field marshal in the German army. He now stood well positioned to drive the British back into Egypt.

Many wondered how Rommel had accomplished such a feat. He later explained that the North African desert lent itself ideally to the mobile offensive tactics of the panzers. It was perfect for panzers, "for whose employment the flat and obstruction-free desert offered hitherto undreamed-of possibilities. It was the only theatre where the theory and principles of motorized and tank warfare could be applied fully and developed further. It was the only arena in which the pure tank battle between major formations could be fought."[6] As Rommel stood poised on the Egyptian frontier, he also stood at the high point of his military career.

After the fall of Tobruk, the British withdrew first to a line at Mersa Matruh, well into Egypt, and then back to the El Alamein Line. El Alamein represented the last-ditch defense of Alexandria. Rommel continued to press forward and arrived at El Alamein on July 1. Running short of supplies and weakened by RAF attacks along the way, he could not penetrate the British defenses in the First Battle of El Alamein. The fighting ended in a standoff on July 27.

Meanwhile, Winston Churchill sent Lieutenant General Bernard L. Montgomery to Egypt to take command of the British Eighth Army. Montgomery began at once to reorganize and retrain his army. Sacking officers and arranging for closer air support, he dedicated himself and his army to driving Rommel out of North Africa. "Here we will stand and fight; there can be no further withdrawal,"[7] he told his officers and men. At Churchill's request, U.S. President Franklin D. Roosevelt sent Sherman tanks and self-propelled artillery to aid Montgomery. A second legendary figure was about to gain fame in the deserts of North Africa.

On October 23, 1942, Montgomery launched his first offensive. In the Second Battle of El Alamein, he faced off against Rommel's Panzer Army with some 195,000 troops, 1,029 tanks, and 2,311 artillery pieces. To meet his challenge, Rommel's forces fielded 104,000 men, 520 tanks, and 1,219 artillery weapons. Montgomery elected to fight a "crumbling" battle. Switching the

General Montgomery, popularly known as "Monty," took command of the British Eighth Army in August 1942.

Under Monty's leadership, the Eighth Army played a key role in driving Rommel's Afrika Korps out of North Africa.

The Second Battle of El Alamein represented the climax of the Western Desert campaigns and one of the turning points of the war. General Montgomery's forces captured some 8,000 German and 16,000 Italian soldiers in the course of the fighting.

Prisoners captured in the fighting in the El Alamein area.

focus of his attack from point to point along the line, he forced Rommel's armor to react.

Rommel had returned to Germany for treatment of a stomach disorder and was absent for part of the battle. He resumed command of the Panzer Army at dusk on October 25. By then, all his reserves had been committed, and it was too late to make any decisions that might alter the course of battle. In several furious tank battles, Montgomery's Grant, Sherman, and Crusader tanks prevailed over Rommel's Panzer IIIs and IVs.

On November 4, Rommel withdrew to the west with an army now reduced to only 22,000 men. Four days later, he received the very bad news that tens of thousands of American and British troops were pouring ashore at nine different places in Morocco and Algeria. Allied armies both to his west and east were advancing on him. The jaws of an Anglo-American vise were already closing. He later stated the obvious in his diary: "This spelt the end of the army in Africa."[8]

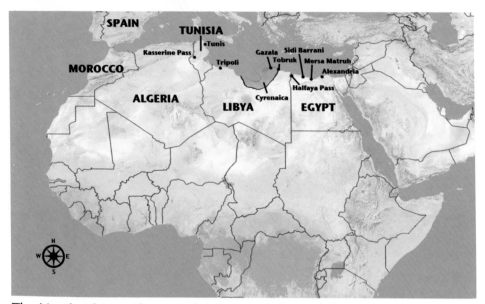

The North African Theater of Operations. General Erwin Rommel arrived in Tripoli in 1941 to take command of the elite German Afrika Korps. For the next two years, he battled Allied forces back and forth across the vast North African deserts. His clever strategies and elusiveness earned him the sobriquet the "Desert Fox." Anglo-American forces advancing on Rommel from both the west and the east finally routed him from North Africa in 1943.

In February 1943, Rommel achieved his last victory in North Africa against green troops of the U.S. II Corps at Kasserine Pass, Tunisia. Rommel's glory days of blitzkrieg triumphs in the North African deserts ended there. Rommel left Tunisia on March 9, 1943. With guts, flair, and cunning, he had written a new chapter in the book of lightning warfare. Hitler rewarded him with Oak Leaves with Swords and Diamonds to his Knight's Cross (a diamond upgrade was the highest order of the medal) and ordered him to take an extended sick leave. The Desert Fox was suffering from severe desert sores (bacterial infections often occurring in hot desert conditions) and deep depression.

Kasserine Pass is a gap in Tunisia's western Dorsal Mountains. There, in February 1943, U.S. soldiers fought their first major battle against the Germans in World War II. The two-mile-wide pass represented the gateway to Tunisia. Tunisia was the last German bastion in North Africa.

Field Marshal Erwin Rommel found himself and the remnants of his Panzer Army being squeezed between advancing Allied armies in the west and in the east. On February 14, the U.S. II Corps took up positions in what was called the Faid Pass. The American presence threatened Rommel's communication lines with the German Fifth Panzer Army to his north. Despite his precarious situation, Rommel decided to attack the U.S. II Corps.

The Americans moved into position about noon. They saw no sign of the enemy and looked forward to a quiet day. Their inexperienced commanders had scattered their tanks among several battalions. This dispersal made it impossible

The 2nd Battalion, 16th Infantry Regiment of the United States Army marches through the Kasserine Pass and on to Kasserine, Tunisia.

to repulse a strong and prolonged enemy tank attack anywhere. And that's what Rommel delivered. Colonel Karl Detzer described the battle's opening:

> First the Stukas dived low, scooting down from the eastern hilltops, machine-gunning our infantry and bombing our artillery positions. Wave after wave, they poured out of the east in the heaviest aerial blow Americans had faced in Africa. Then out of the pass roared the German counterattack. The panzers were manned by Rommel's Afrika Korps veterans, and they smashed through the undermanned Allied forces and sent them reeling.[9]

The Americans scrambled back into Kasserine Pass and dug in. With the aid of British forces and strong air power, the Americans recovered fast. Rommel ran into strong positions and pulled back through the pass on February 23. By then, he had inflicted some 9,000 casualties on the Allies and destroyed 183 Allied tanks. Kasserine Pass marked his last victory in North Africa. The U.S. II Corps later redeemed itself on the way to the capital city of Tunis under General George S. Patton.

Hitler's Wehrmacht (armed forces) used blitzkrieg tactics to defeat Poland in less than a month and forced the fall of France in only six weeks.

When Hitler sought Lebensraum (living space) for Germans in the broad expanses of the Soviet Union, the Wehrmacht enjoyed similar successes on the Eastern Front. Then the icy Russian winter struck and stole the Wehrmacht's lightning.

CHAPTER 4

Operation Barbarossa and the Invasion of the Soviet Union

The Allied armies did not prevail in North Africa by "outfoxing" the Desert Fox. Rather, it was their industrial might—chiefly that of the United States—that succeeded in wearing him down. Rommel could not sustain his blitzkrieg campaigns without a continuing supply of tanks and planes. Had he been equipped with unlimited resources, the course of the desert war might have taken a different turn. That was not to be. Four months after Rommel landed in Tripoli, Hitler launched Operation Barbarossa—the invasion of the Soviet Union—on June 22, 1941. From then on, the bulk of Germany's war resources went to the eastern front.

On that fateful Sunday morning in June, Hitler sent 148 divisions, 3,350 tanks, 7,100 cannon, 2,000 airplanes, and 3 million men rumbling into the Soviet Union. From the Baltic to the Black Sea, mechanized German forces attacked along an 1,800-mile-long front. Hitler hated Communists, but he justified his invasion policy on the need for *Lebensraum*—living space for Germans in the vast fertile plains of western Russia. His words at a briefing for his officers suggested something much more evil. "Wiping out the very power of Russia to exist! That is the goal!"[1]

Hitler issued his war plan for the Soviet Union as Directive 21. He later renamed it Barbarossa after German king and Holy Roman emperor Frederick I, whose family name was Barbarossa. Frederick was drowned while leading the Third Crusade in 1190. Legend held that he would rise from a deathlike sleep and lead Germany in the conquest of Europe. As yet, Frederick has failed to awaken. Hitler received no help from the dead. Instead, he gambled everything on the Wehrmacht and the blitzkrieg capabilities that had served

him well in Poland and Western Europe. This time, however, his plan was flawed.

Hitler had wanted to launch his invasion in May, but fighting in the Balkans upset his timing. He was forced to temporarily divert troops to the Balkans and Greece. Putting down local resistance moved his schedule closer to the Russian winter. Several of Hitler's top military advisers warned him against a late start. Hitler would have none of it. He felt sure he could conquer the Soviet Union in six months. "We have only to kick in the door," he said, "and the whole rotten structure will come crashing down."[2] Barbarossa began a month late under the overall command of Field Marshal Walther von Brauchitsch.

Hitler's plan called for Army Groups North, Center, and South to attack all at once along the vast eastern front. Starting from Finland and Poland, Army Group North was to attack the three Baltic nations of Estonia, Latvia, and Lithuania. It would then drive on to Leningrad. Army Group Center was to start from East Prussia and Poland and thrust eastward to envelop Minsk and Smolensk in turn. From Czechoslovakia, Army Group South would assault the Ukraine and advance toward the Caucasus Mountains. A tactical air force would support each army group.

In the early going, the Germans met with astonishing success everywhere. By July 2, they had destroyed 1,000 Soviet aircraft and captured 150,000 Russian soldiers, along with 1,200 tanks and 600 big guns. The Nazis were elated. The next day, German chief of staff General Franz Halder wrote in his diary: "It is probably not an exaggeration to say that the campaign against Russia has been won in fourteen days."[3] And so it seemed.

In the second week in July, Heinz Guderian took another 500,000 prisoners. Smolensk fell on August 5, giving up 310,000 more Russians. Kiev surrendered on September 16 with 500,000 more. Hitler's blitzkrieg rumbled on toward the Soviet capital of Moscow. It appeared invincible and unstoppable. Then reality set in. The rapid advance across a broad front had spread the German ranks dangerously thin. Their exposed flanks became vulnerable to counterattacks, which the Soviets began to mount with great skill.

To make matters worse, the Germans had vastly underestimated the strength of the Soviet army. "We misjudged the combat strength and combat

efficiency of the enemy as well as our own troops," conceded Army Group Center's chief of staff, General Hans von Greiffenberg. "At the beginning we reckoned with some 200 enemy divisions. We have already identified 360. When a dozen of them are destroyed, the Russians throw in another dozen."[4] Furthermore, the Soviets built 6,590 tanks that year, compared to only 3,750 by the Germans.

Soviet forces began to gather between Smolensk and Moscow. The German High Command urged Hitler to concentrate his forces in the center and drive toward Moscow without delay. Hitler refused, eyeing instead Leningrad in the north and Stalingrad in the south. He considered them to be the twin "holy cities of Communism."[5] Their fall, he believed, would cause a Soviet collapse. Moreover, he craved the industry, oil, and grain fields of the south. The psychological and economical aspects of Hitler's offensive caused him to lose sight of his original goal—the destruction of the Soviet army.

Hitler's strategy contained numerous other flaws. After surrounding huge numbers of Soviet soldiers, his panzers were forced to slow down and help the following infantry capture or kill the enemy masses. Then the rains came, turning the few dirt roads to mud and rendering the adjacent fields impassable. The blitzkrieg bogged down.

Logistics—that is, the supplies and services needed to keep Hitler's war machine moving—became a huge problem. The Germans launched Barbarossa with only a month's supply of diesel fuel for the panzers. Supplies had to be shipped from German depots over muddy roads or via primitive railroads for more than 300 miles. Soviet railroads had to be converted to the German gauge (distance between rails). Each panzer division required 300 tons of supplies a day to remain operational. Some got as little as seventy tons. Field Marshal Gunther von Blumentritt, chief of staff of the German Fourth Army, later described the miseries of Russian combat vividly:

> The infantryman slithers in the mud. . . . All wheeled vehicles sink up to their axles in the slime. Even tractors can move only with great difficulty. A large portion of our heavy artillery was soon stuck fast. . . . The strain that all this caused our already exhausted troops can perhaps be imagined.[6]

Reduced to a slog, and irrespective of the hardships, the blitzkrieg pressed on.

On October 2, Field Marshal Fedor von Bock's Army Group Center launched fourteen panzer divisions and three infantry armies in Operation Typhoon. The Russian winter struck amid Bock's final thrust at Moscow. First came the October rains, followed by thaw and more mud, and finally by falling snow and subzero temperatures. Tankers had to light fires under their panzers to start them. Hitler's generals recommended a halt until spring. Hitler said to continue the advance over frozen turf. German soldiers struggled forward through rain and snow, ill-clothed and ill-equipped for plunging temperatures.

By November 27, Guderian's panzers drew within nineteen miles of Moscow. The Kremlin's gilded towers loomed into view. German hopes ran

Map of Operation Barbarossa. Barbarossa was the code name for the German offensive against the Soviet Union in June 1941. Hitler attacked the Soviets with 148 divisions, supported by thousands of aircraft, tanks, and cannon. The Germans struck all along an 1,800-mile front that stretched from the Baltic Sea to the Black Sea.

high. But temperatures dropped far below zero. Automatic weapons froze and could not fire. And Soviet forces began to counterattack all along the front. Von Bock proposed a fifty-mile retreat to a more defensible line. Hitler said no and ordered his armies to stand fast. They could not.

On December 6, 1941, Marshal Georgi Zhukov unleashed a great Soviet offensive along the 200-mile Moscow front. Unexpectedly, 100 Soviet divisions struck the Germans so hard and fast they never fully recovered. "The myth of the invincibility of the German Army was broken,"[7] General Franz Halder noted later. More surprisingly, the Japanese bombed Pearl Harbor the next day. On December 11, Hitler, honoring an earlier agreement with Japan, declared war on the United States—a decision he would regret.

Hitler's mighty war machine bogged down within sight of Moscow in the snow and frigid temperatures of a Russian winter.

Soviet offensive in Moscow in December 1941.

Heinz Guderian flew to Hitler's field headquarters in East Prussia, about 500 miles from the fighting. Guderian was one of the few commanders not afraid to stand up to Hitler. He wanted to persuade Hitler to fall back before it was too late. Hitler refused Guderian's advice. "One final heave and we shall triumph,"[8] he said. Guderian returned to the front and—on his own—ordered his panzers to withdraw. He later explained:

> Only he who saw the endless expanse of Russian snow during this winter of our misery and felt the icy wind that blew across it, burying in snow every object in its path; who drove for hour after hour through that no-man's-land only at last to find too thin shelter with insufficiently clothed, half-starved men; and who also saw by contrast the well-fed, warmly clad and fresh Siberians, fully equipped for winter fighting . . . can truly judge the events which now occurred.[9]

For acting against orders to save his panzers, Hitler dismissed Guderian, effective on Christmas Day, 1941.

Zhukov's offensive drove the Germans back anywhere from 50 to 200 miles from Moscow. They would never again come so close to the Soviet capital. After the Soviets lifted the German siege of Stalingrad in February 1943, Hitler called on the Wehrmacht for one more battle of annihilation outside Kursk in central Russia. That summer, the Soviets broke the will of the Germans in the greatest tank battle in history. Thereafter, the Soviets would gradually force Hitler's once-proud Wehrmacht to retreat along all fronts.

The mass of Soviet troops, tanks, and aircraft turned Hitler's lightning war into a humbling backward crawl. And on the western front, the military situation soon turned equally grave for the Germans. On June 6, 1944, Allied forces landed on the beaches of Normandy, France.

Kursk

By the spring of 1943, Soviet attackers had forced a large bulge in the German lines in the south-central sector of the eastern front. Located outside the Russian city of Kursk, the bulge was aptly named the Kursk salient. It measured 60 miles deep by 110 miles wide. Hitler, who was growing increasingly desperate with each new defeat, decided to pinch off the salient. He saw this action as a great battle of annihilation. For this purpose, he assembled a new force of 500,000 men. The force included seventeen

Hitler makes a front-line visit to von Manstein's headquarters in Zaporozhye, Ukraine.

panzer divisions equipped with the new Tiger tank. Hitler called the impending battle Operation Citadel. It was set to begin as soon as the spring thaws ended and the muddy ground dried out.

Unknown to the Germans, Soviet intelligence had warned Marshal Zhukov of the German plan. To meet the challenge, Zhukov put together a force of 1.3 million men and a huge number of T-34 medium tanks and KV-1 heavy tanks. He laid thick minefields on stretches suitable to German tanks, and he set in huge batteries of artillery and rockets.

Waffen-SS Panzergrenadiers discus an offensive action with a Tiger 1 commander in Kursk.

The Battle of Kursk began on July 5, 1943. Field Marshals Erich von Manstein and Gunther von Kluge launched the attack. They pressed forward with about 2,400 tanks and assault guns and 2,500 aircraft. Zhukov countered with more than 3,000 tanks and assault guns and 2,600 aircraft. The battle blew hot and cold. It reached a climax in a giant tank battle on July 12. Some 700 tanks of the German Fourth Panzer Army clashed with 850 tanks of the Soviet Fifth Guards Tank Army. Both sides lost about 1,500 tanks in the largest tank battle in history. The battle was inconclusive, but the Soviets seized the initiative on the eastern front and kept it for the rest of the war.

Left to right: Lt. Gen. Omar N. Bradley, General Dwight D. Eisenhower, and Lt. Gen. George S. Patton.

General Eisenhower served as supreme commander of the Allied invasion forces in Europe in 1944 to 1945. As Twelfth Army Group commander, General Bradley headed the largest field force ever commanded by an American general. General Patton's Third Army covered more ground and took more prisoners than any other Allied force.

War—Then and Now

In March 1944, Lieutenant General George S. Patton was named commander of the newly formed U.S. Third Army. On July 4, exactly one month after the Normandy landings, he arrived at Avranches (ahv-RAHNSH), France. The Third Army became operational against the Germans on August 1. Beginning that day, Patton and his army led the breakout of American forces from the Normandy beachhead at Saint-Lô. Patton drove through the gap at Avranches, sweeping west, south, and east, isolating the French province of Brittany. At Le Mans, he was directed northward toward Argentan.

In desperation, Hitler ordered a panzer attack to cut off Patton at Avranches. The attack came on August 6. Field Marshal Gunther von Kluge ordered Lieutenant General Fritz Bayerlein's once-proud Panzer Lehr Division to hold to the last man. "Out in front everyone is holding out. Everyone," Bayerlein replied with unchecked anger. "Not a single man is leaving his post. They are lying silently in their foxholes, for they are dead. You understand? Dead . . . The Panzer Lehr Division is annihilated!"[1]

General Alan Brooke, chief of the British general staff, commented on Hitler's failure to withdraw when he had the chance: "He's worth 40 divisions to us."[2] The Allies had long since seized control of the air. Hitler was learning the hard way that blitzkrieg will not work without air superiority. His lightning war was dying a slow death. He could only watch while the Americans stole page after page from his book of blitzkrieg tactics.

On August 13, Patton's Third Army trapped some 100,000 Germans at what later became known as the Falaise-Argentan Gap. Patton then turned and drove eastward until his army ran out of gas at the Saar River in late August. Supply services found it difficult to keep pace with the fast-moving

Patton. The Third Army continued its eastward dash in September and stopped at the fortified German frontier.

On December 16, Hitler, in still another desperate move, launched his Ardennes Offensive, better known as the Battle of the Bulge. A last-gasp, blitz-krieg-style German attack succeeded in penetrating the Allied lines and forming a salient (bulge) roughly 60 miles deep by 40 miles wide. During their surprise offensive, the Germans isolated the U.S. 101st Airborne Division at Bastogne (baa-STOHN), Belgium, and demanded its surrender. Brigadier General Anthony McAuliffe, commander of the 101st, replied with an economy of words: "Nuts!"[3]

Patton raced to the rescue of McAuliffe's division. In less than a week, he moved almost a quarter million men and thousands of trucks and tanks from fifty to seventy miles to lift the siege at Bastogne. His remarkable achieve-

Adolf Hitler and German officials view the rubble in a German city in 1944.

The massive Allied night and daylight bombing campaigns were devastating. Despite the widespread destruction of German cities, Hitler launched a last-gasp offensive in the Ardennes in December 1944.

ment was just one of many reasons why Field Marshal Gerd von Rundstedt told his Allied captors after the war, "Patton was your best."[4]

The Allies wiped out the "bulge" in late January 1945 and pressed their advance into Germany. Patton led the way, pushing his army aggressively through the Rhineland and across Germany in a blitzkrieg of his own. His army was camped in Czechoslovakia when he was ordered to stop at war's end. When it came to blitzkrieg, no one did it better than Patton.

Patton studied military history with a passion for perfecting his professional skills. He read everything about war and warriors he could lay his hands on. From Alexander the Great to Heinz Guderian, he devoured the teachings of those who practiced the art of war—and he applied the lessons he learned to the battlefield.

This division achieved renown for its staunch resistance while under siege by Germans at a critical road junction at the Belgian town of Bastogne in December 1944.

American paratroopers of the 101st Airborne Division display a Nazi flag captured in a village assault.

After World War II, and before the wars in Iraq, the United States fought a major war in Korea and another in Vietnam. U.S. and United Nations forces conducted several determined offensives in the rice paddies and mountains of Korea. Offensive action in Vietnam was confined largely to small-scale "search and destroy" missions in the hills and jungles. In both wars, the United States controlled the skies, and its fighting forces were far better supplied, armed, and equipped than those of the enemy. But in both wars, rugged terrain ruled out the successful use of blitzkrieg-style offensives.

In war, the strategies and tactics employed depend on the terrain and the situation. Thus, it is no coincidence that, after World War II, blitzkrieg-style offensives have been limited to desert warfare. Rommel had it right—the desert is ideal for panzers.

"What Patton and Rommel practiced during World War II is, fifty years later, an accepted means of successfully waging war," observes Carlo D'Este, one of Patton's many biographers. "The success of Israel's tank victories in the desert during the various Arab-Israeli wars, and those of the Allies in the 1991 Gulf War, fully attest to their legacy."[5] (D'Este's observation applies equally as well to the more recent 2003 Iraq War.)

On August 1, 1990, Iraq invaded Kuwait. Iraqi dictator Saddam Hussein claimed that Kuwait was illegally draining oil from an Iraqi oil field. Actually, Hussein wanted to acquire the rich Kuwaiti oil fields. The United Nations (UN) demanded Iraq's withdrawal by January 15, 2001. In the meantime, the United States and its allies formed a coalition of thirty-eight nations to enforce the UN demand, if necessary. When Hussein ignored the UN deadline, the coalition acted.

The Persian Gulf War of 1991 began on the night of January 16. A massive U.S.-led air offensive struck Iraq and continued throughout the war. On March 24, a powerful, blitzkrieg-like ground offensive ended the brief war in seventy-two hours. Iraq withdrew from Kuwait, but it did not meet UN cease-fire terms for the destruction of its research facilities for weapons of mass destruction (WMDs). Saddam's refusal to comply with UN terms led directly to another war twelve years later.

Like the earlier Gulf War, the Iraq War of 2003 began with a massive aerial bombardment to "shock and awe" the enemy. Air-raid sirens in Baghdad

signaled the start of hostilities at 5:30 A.M. on March 20. At the same time, U.S. soldiers and marines entered Iraq from Kuwait and advanced 350 miles—blitzkrieg-style—to Baghdad in twenty-one days. The Americans and their allies—chiefly British—found no WMDs, but they ousted the ruthless Saddam Hussein from power.

The question of whether the U.S.-led invasion of Iraq was right or just must await the verdict of history. What both wars in Iraq clearly demonstrated, however, is that the blitzkrieg principles used by Guderian, Rommel, and Patton in World War II remain just as deadly and effective in today's warfare. Changes have occurred since then, of course. Militarists, for example, now refer to blitzkrieg as "rapid dominance." Soldiers are now better trained and equipped. And weaponry has become more powerful and sophisticated. Nonetheless, old soldiers would likely recognize today's shock-and-awe campaigns as yesterday's blitzkrieg offensives.

Perhaps the major difference in the lightning-fast campaigns of then and now lies in the province of intent. The main goal of Hitler's blitzkrieg was to wipe out the enemy. This required deep penetration of the enemy's defenses. Using speed, surprise, and the force of combined arms, large pockets of enemy troops would be isolated, surrounded, and killed. Today, the means remain similar, but the end goal has shifted. Destruction of the enemy's command, control, communications, and intelligence systems is key. This is designed to erode the enemy's ability and will to fight. Thus, today's emphasis is to force a quick surrender with a minimum loss of life on both sides.

On the surface, the objective of modern warfare may seem more humane than the aims of yesteryear's conflicts. Modern technology has reduced what military people call "collateral damage" (unintentional damage or death due to errant bombs or shells). But no war can be correctly described as humane. To paraphrase General William T. Sherman, war is—always was, and ever will be—hell. The world can only hope that someday humankind can find a way to end all war for all time—including *Blitzkrieg!*

By September 1944, Hitler knew he was losing the war. His empire was toppling all around him. He needed a miracle to turn the war around. At a meeting with several of his top generals, he laid out a plan to seize victory from impending defeat. Code-named Watch on the Rhine, his plan called for another offensive through the Allied lines in the Ardennes region of Belgium and France.

Hitler's aim was to seize the Belgian port of Antwerp. At the same time, he planned to isolate and exterminate the Allied armies north of the corridor his offensive would form. Hitler's Ardennes Offensive—later called the Battle of the Bulge—began on December 16, 1944.

Hitler's surprise thrust through the Ardennes involved three panzer armies—the Fifth, Seventh, and General Josef "Sepp" Dietrich's crack Sixth Panzer Army. Of his assignment, Dietrich later wrote: "All I had to do was cross the river, capture Brussels, and then go on and take the port of Antwerp. The

American soldiers take up defensive positions in the Ardennes during the Battle of the Bulge.

snow was waist-deep and there wasn't room to deploy four tanks abreast, let alone six Panzer divisions. It didn't get light till eight and was dark again at four and my tanks can't fight at night. And all this at Christmas time!"[6] He failed to mention that it was also the coldest winter in Europe in fifty-four years.

Hitler's desperate gamble succeeded in driving a salient in the Allied lines some sixty miles deep and forty miles wide. The bulge gave name to the battle, but the panzers did not break through. Their offensive fell short of capturing vital fuel dumps essential to sustaining the drive. The Allies rallied and hammered out the bump in their lines in the largest battle ever fought by the U.S. Army. Of the 600,000 U.S. soldiers involved, the Battle of the Bulge claimed 80,000 casualties—roughly 20,000 killed, 40,000 wounded, and 20,000 captured. It was Hitler's last blitzkrieg.

Chronology

1933		Adolf Hitler becomes chancellor (head of state) in Germany; the Third Reich (empire) is established.
1939		Germany invades Poland on September 1; World War II begins.
1940	*April*	Germany invades Denmark and Norway.
	May	Germany invades the Low Countries and France; British and French forces evacuate from Dunkirk, France.
	June	France falls to Hitler's Wehrmacht; Italy enters the war on Germany's side.
	July–October	The Royal Air Force defeats the Luftwaffe in the Battle of Britain.
1941	*February*	Rommel and the Afrika Korps arrive in Libya.
	March	Rommel launches first desert campaign against the British.
	April	Rommel recovers Libyan land lost by Italians.
	June	Hitler launches Operation Barbarossa, the invasion of the Soviet Union; Rommel takes Tobruk.
	July	Rommel fights to a standoff in the First Battle of El Alamein.
	November	Wehrmacht is stopped at the gates of Moscow.
	December	Soviets launch offensive in front of Moscow; Japanese bomb Pearl Harbor.
1942	*October–November*	Montgomery defeats Rommel in the Second Battle of El Alamein.
1943	*February*	Rommel defeats U.S. forces at Kasserine Pass, Tunisia; Soviets lift German siege at Stalingrad.
	July	Soviets seize initiative after the Battle of Kursk.
1944	*June*	Allies land at Normandy, France.
	August	Patton leads Allied breakout at Avranches; traps 100,000 Germans at the Falaise-Argentan Gap.
	December	Hitler launches Ardennes offensive (Battle of the Bulge); Patton lifts German siege of Bastogne.
1945	*January*	Allies beat back the "bulge" in their lines in the Ardennes and resume their offensive.
	May	Germany surrenders on May 7; World War II ends in Europe.
	August	Japan surrenders to Allies.
	September	Japan signs surrender documents; World War II ends in Asia and the Pacific.
1950–53		UN forces fight North Korean/Chinese forces to a standoff in Korea.
1965–75		U.S. forces and allies engage Vietcong and North Vietnamese regular forces in the Vietnam War.
1990		Iraq invades Kuwait.
1991		Coalition armies force Iraqi withdrawal from Kuwait in the Persian Gulf War.
2003		Coalition forces invade Iraq and topple regime of Saddam Hussein.
2007		Coalition forces continue to battle insurgents in Iraq.

Timeline in History

1870	Prussians defeat French in the Franco-Prussian War.
1898	United States defeats Spain in the Spanish-American War.
1900	Boxers, members of a Chinese secret society, stage rebellion against Europeans.
1904	Russo-Japanese War begins.
1905	Japan defeats Russia; Russo-Japanese War ends.
1914	World War I begins between Germany and the Allies—chiefly Great Britain and France, and later the United States.
1917	Bolsheviks (Communists) revolt in Russia.
1918	Allies defeat Germany; World War I ends.
1919	Allies impose harsh peace terms on Germany in the Treaty of Versailles.
1921	Russian civil war ends.
1933	Hitler and Nazis take power in Germany.
1936	Spanish Civil War begins in July and lasts until March 1939.
1939–1945	World War II is fought between the Allies (Great Britain, France, the Soviet Union, and the United States) and the Axis powers (Germany, Italy, and Japan).
1945	United Nations is formed in San Francisco.
1946	Cold war between the Soviet Union and Western powers begins.
1957	Soviet Union launches *Sputnik*, the first satellite to orbit the Earth.
1962	United States confronts the Soviet Union in the Cuban Missile Crisis.
1969	U.S. astronaut Neil Armstrong becomes the first man to walk on the moon.
1991	Soviet Union dissolves; cold war ends.
2007	World leaders press the United Nations to deploy promised peacekeeping troops to Sudan to halt the genocide in Darfur.

Chapter Notes

Chapter 1. Resurrection

1. German Culture, *Nazi Party*, http://www.germanculture.com.ua/library/weekly/aa012400b.htm

2. Brenda Ralph Lewis, *Hitler Youth: The Hitlerjugend in War and Peace 1933–1945* (St. Paul, Minnesota: Zenith Press, 2000), p. 105.

3. Robert Leckie, *The Wars of America*, vol. II (New York: HarperPerennial, 1993), p. 686.

4. Louis L. Snyder, *Encyclopedia of the Third Reich* (New York: Paragon House, 1989), p. 116.

5. William L. Shirer, *The Rise and Fall of the Third Reich: A History of Nazi Germany* (New York: Simon and Schuster, 1960), p. 599.

6. Matthew Cooper, *The German Army 1933–1945: Its Political and Military Failure*, Military Book Club edition (USA: Scarborough House, undated), p. 116.

7. Trevor N. Dupuy, *A Genius for War: The German Army and General Staff, 1807–1945* (Garden City, New York: Military Book Club, 2002), p. 257.

8. Charles Townshend, ed., *The Oxford Illustrated History of Modern War* (New York: Oxford University Press, 1997), p. 194.

9. James S. Corum, *The Roots of Blitzkrieg: Hans von Seeckt and German Military Reform* (Lawrence, Kansas: University Press of Kansas, 1992), p. xvii.

Chapter 2. Operation Yellow and the Fall of France

1. Louis L. Snyder, *Encyclopedia of the Third Reich* (New York: Paragon House, 1989), p. 111.

2. Norman Polmar and Thomas B. Allen, *World War II: The Encyclopedia of the War Years 1941–1945* (New York: Random House, 1996), p. 307.

3. Ronald E. Powaski, *Lightning War: Blitzkrieg in the West, 1940* (Edison, New Jersey: Castle Books, 2006), pp.144–45.

4. Erwin Rommel, *The Rommel Papers*, edited by B. H. Liddell Hart, with Lucie-Maria Rommel, Manfred Rommel, and General Fritz

Bayerlein, translated by Paul Findlay (New York: Da Capo Press, 1953), p. 34.

Chapter 3. The Desert Fox in North Africa
1. Norman Polmar and Thomas B. Allen, *World War II: The Encyclopedia of the War Years 1941–1945* (New York: Random House, 1996), p. 588.
2. Ibid., p. 589.
3. Erwin Rommel, *The Rommel Papers*, edited by B. H. Liddell Hart, with Lucie-Maria Rommel, Manfred Rommel, and General Fritz Bayerlein, translated by Paul Findlay (New York: Da Capo Press, 1953), p. 98.
4. Christer Jörgensen, *Rommel's Panzers: Rommel and the Panzer Forces of the Blitzkrieg 1940–1942* (St. Paul, Minnesota: Zenith Press, 2003), p. 83.
5. Polmar and Allen, p. 590.
6. Jörgensen, p. 129.
7. Polmar and Allen, p. 590.
8. Rommel, p. 345.
9. Karl Detzer, *Illustrated History of World War II*, "Operation Torch" (Pleasantville, New York: Reader's Digest Association, 1978), p. 309.

Chapter 4. Operation Barbarossa and the Invasion of the Soviet Union
1. C. L. Sulzberger, *World War II* (New York: American Heritage, 1985), p. 117.

2. Robert Leckie, *The Wars of America*, vol. II (New York: HarperPerennial, 1993), p. 723.
3. Ibid., p. 724.
4. Sidney C. Moody Jr., *War in Europe* (Novato, California: Presidio Press, 1993), p. 59.
5. Leckie, p. 724.
6. William L. Shirer, *Illustrated History of World War II*, "The Germans Invade Russia" (Pleasantville, New York: Reader's Digest Association, 1978), p. 265.
7. Sulzberger, p. 125.
8. Shirer, p. 268.
9. Ibid., p. 265.

Chapter 5. War—Then and Now
1. Sidney C. Moody Jr., *War in Europe* (Novato, California: Presidio Press, 1993), p. 139.
2. Ibid.
3. Robert Leckie, *The Wars of America*, vol. II (New York: HarperPerennial, 1993), p. 816.
4. Martin Blumenson, *Patton: The Man Behind the Legend, 1885–1945* (New York: Quill/William Morrow, 1985), p. 296.
5. Carlo D'Este, *Patton: A Genius for War* (New York: HarperCollins, 1995), p. 811.
6. Ian V. Hogg, *The Hutchinson Dictionary of Battles* (Oxford, England: Helicon Publishing, 1998), p. 27.

Glossary

blitzkrieg (BLITZ-kreeg)—German for "lightning war."

Crusader tank—Mk III Crusader, medium British tank; formed the main equipment of British armored divisions fighting in the North African desert campaigns.

Grant tank—M3 General Grant tank, the first U.S. medium tank; used in the early part of World War II until succeeded by the improved M4 Sherman tank.

Hurricane—Hawker Hurricane; single-engined British fighter plane that was largely responsible for the Royal Air Force's victory over the Luftwaffe during the Battle of Britain in the summer of 1940.

Junkers Ju-88—a twin-engined civil aircraft converted for military use; it was used as a bomber, fighter, night fighter, destroyer, tank buster, reconnaissance plane, and other applications as dictated by Berlin.

KV-1 tank—Soviet heavy tank, heavily armored and almost invulnerable to German antitank guns.

Lebensraum (LAY-benz-rahm)—German for "living space"; Hitler used the Germans' need for more living space to justify his occupation of much of Europe.

Messerschmitt Me (Bf) 109—German premier single-engined fighter plane at the start of World War II; it remained in active combat throughout the war.

Nazi (NAHT-see)—a member of the German National Socialist Party that controlled Germany from 1933 to 1945; a contraction of *Nationalsozialist*.

Panzer III—medium tank that formed the bulk of German panzer divisions in the early years of World War II; *panzer* means "armor" in German, a term usually applied to tanks.

Panzer IV—originally conceived by Heinz Guderian as a heavy support tank for Panzer IIIs, it became the workhorse of panzer divisions in the later years of World War II.

Sherman tank—M4 General Sherman tank, the standard U.S. Army and Marine Corps medium tank in World War II from 1943 on; considered by many to have been the most successful tank of the war.

Spitfire—Supermarine Spitfire; premier single-engined British fighter plane in 1940; it became the symbol of British resistance against the Nazis.

Stuka (STOO-kuh)—Junkers Ju-87, a gull-winged, single-engined dive-bomber with fixed landing gear; the main support aircraft for German blitzkrieg campaigns against Poland, France, and the Soviet Union; a contraction of *Sturzkampfflugzeug*, German for "dive-bomber."

T-34 tank—Soviet medium tank, the mainstay of the Soviet tank corps; some 40,000 T-34s were produced between 1940 and 1945.

Tiger tank—German heavy tank that first entered action around Leningrad in World War II.

Further Reading

For Young Adults

Gavin, Philip. *World War II in Europe.* Farmington Hills, Michigan: Lucent Books, 2004.

Nishi, Dennis. *Weapons of War: World War II.* Farmington Hills, Michigan: Thomson Gale, 2000.

Rice, Earle Jr. *Erwin J. E. Rommel.* New York: Chelsea House, 2003.

Souter, Gerry. *Battle Tanks: Power in the Field.* Berkeley Heights, New Jersey: Enslow, 2006.

Stein, R. Conrad. *World War II in Europe: America Goes to War.* Berkeley Heights, New Jersey: Enslow, 2000.

Works Consulted

Barnett, Correlli, ed. *Hitler's Generals.* New York: Quill/William Morrow, 1989.

Blitzkrieg: In Their Own Words: First-hand Accounts from German Soldiers 1939–1940. Translated by Alan Bance. St. Paul, Minnesota: Zenith Press, 2005.

Blumenson, Martin. *Patton: The Man Behind the Legend, 1885–1945.* New York: Quill/William Morrow, 1985.

Chamberlain, Peter, and Hilary Doyle. *Encyclopedia of German Tanks of World War Two.* Revised edition. London: Arms and Armour, 2000.

Cooper, Matthew. *The German Army 1933–1945: Its Political and Military Failure.* Military Book Club edition. USA: Scarborough House, undated.

Corum, James S. *The Roots of Blitzkrieg: Hans von Seeckt and German Military Reform.* Lawrence, Kansas: University Press of Kansas, 1992.

D'Este, Carlo. *Patton: A Genius for War.* New York: HarperCollins, 1995.

Dupuy, Trevor N. *A Genius for War: The German Army and General Staff,*

1807–1945. Garden City, New York: Military Book Club, 2002.

Fowler, Will. *The Atlas of Eastern Front Battles.* New York: Military Book Club/Bookspan, 2002.

Fraser, David. *Knight's Cross: A Life of Field Marshal Erwin Rommel.* New York: HarperPerennial, 1994.

Gilbert, Adrian. *The Encyclopedia of Warfare: From Earliest Times to the Present Day.* Guilford, Connecticut: Lyons Press/Globe Pequot Press, 2002.

Hogg, Ian V. *The Hutchinson Dictionary of Battles.* Oxford, England: Helicon Publishing, 1998.

Irving, David. *Rommel: The Trail of the Fox.* Ware, Hertfordshire, England: Wordsworth Editions, 1999.

Jörgensen, Christer. *Rommel's Panzers: Rommel and the Panzer Forces of the Blitzkrieg 1940–1942.* St. Paul, Minnesota: Zenith Press, 2003.

Kaufmann, J. E., and H. W. Kaufmann. *Hitler's Blitzkrieg Campaigns: The Invasion and Defense of Western Europe, 1939–1940.* Conshohocken, Pennsylvania: Combined Publishing, 1993.

Leckie, Robert. *The Wars of America.* Vol. II. New York: HarperPerennial, 1993.

Lewis, Brenda Ralph. *Hitler Youth: The Hitlerjugend in War and Peace 1933–1945.* St. Paul, Minnesota: Zenith Press, 2000.

Lucas, James. *Hitler's Enforcers: Leaders of the German War Machine 1939–1945.* London: Arms and Armour, 1996.

Mitcham, Samuel W. Jr. *Triumphant Fox: Erwin Rommel and the Rise of the Afrika Korps.* New York: Cooper Square Press, 2000.

Moody, Sidney C. Jr. *War in Europe.* Novato, California: Presidio Press, 1993.

Polmar, Norman, and Thomas B. Allen. *World War II: The Encyclopedia of the War Years 1941–1945.* New York: Random House, 1996.

Powaski, Ronald E. *Lightning War: Blitzkrieg in the West, 1940.* Edison, New Jersey: Castle Books, 2006.

Reader's Digest. *Illustrated History of World War II.* Pleasantville, New York: Reader's Digest Association, 1978.

Rommel, Erwin. *The Rommel Papers.* Edited by B. H. Liddell Hart, with Lucie-Maria Rommel, Manfred Rommel, and General Fritz Bayerlein. Translated by Paul Findlay. New York: Da Capo Press, 1953.

Shirer, William L. *The Rise and Fall of the Third Reich: A History of Nazi Germany.* New York: Simon and Schuster, 1960.

Snyder, Louis L. *Encyclopedia of the Third Reich.* New York: Paragon House, 1989.

Stephenson, Michael, ed. *Battlegrounds: Geography and the History of Warfare.* Washington, D.C.: National Geographic Society, 2003.

Sulzberger, C. L. *World War II.* New York: American Heritage, 1985.

Townshend, Charles, ed. *The Oxford Illustrated History of Modern War.* New York: Oxford University Press, 1997.

Young, Desmond. *Rommel: The Desert Fox.* New York: Quill/William Morrow, 1987.

On the Internet

Eyewitness to History: "Blitzkrieg, 1940" http://www.eyewitnesstohistory.com/pfblitzkrieg.htm

German Culture: *Nazi Party* http://www.germanculture.com.ua/library/weekly/aa012400b.htm

Index